HOW TO
SAVE 5000

This Year - and Every Year!

REDUCE YOUR OUTGOINGS WITHOUT
REDUCING YOUR LIFESTYLE

James O'Donovan

Published by
OAK TREE PRESS, 19 Rutland Street, Cork, Ireland
www.oaktreepress.com
www.HowToSave5000.com

A catalogue record of this book is available from the British
Library.

ISBN 978 1 78119 043 2 (Paperback)
ISBN 978 1 78119 044 9 (ePub)
ISBN 978 1 78119 045 6 (Kindle)

Printed in Ireland by SPRINT-print Ltd

Contents

1: Introduction

HOW TO SAVE 5000: *This Year - and Every Year!*
will teach you how to save €5,000 (or pounds or dollars or
whatever currency you use wherever you live) a year just
by changing some of your spending habits but without
making any major lifestyle changes.

Everyone wants to improve their personal finances in
any way they can. The most obvious way to do this is to
increase what's coming in – get a job with a higher salary.
This option is not always possible and a separate book
could be written on that topic. The only alternative then is
to reduce what's going out and to keep more of your
money quite simply by spending less of it.

Sounds obvious? Yes, and it is.

Sounds impossible? Yes, but it isn't.

Saving is Simple

Saving €5,000 a year on an average salary can be achieved
without making major lifestyle changes. It is possible to
maintain your current lifestyle, within reason, and spend

less money at the same time. This book will teach you ways to spend your money smarter – for example, by switching utility providers and getting the same service for less money, or by buying a car mug and making coffee each morning before leaving the house instead buying it at the local convenience store. By following the techniques outlined in this book on an ongoing basis, you will change your spending habits and could end up saving literally thousands over the years.

The Cumulative Effect of Savings

That is because savings must be considered *cumulatively*. So, even if you only save €100 once-off on one of your utility bills by switching providers, over 10 years that modest saving is worth €1,000 because assuming that provider remains the cheapest, you continue to save €100 each year against your original bill. Just picture someone handing you €1,000 cash in 10 years' time simply because you switched to their service 10 years earlier.

And even if you just manage to save €2,500 a year (quite achievable), then you can see what that adds up to over 10 years. That is the beauty of making the techniques in this book a permanent habit.

Change Your Habits

This book lists nine spending categories and analyses each to show how savings can be made. Regardless of your current situation, whether working or unemployed, house owner or renting, there are numerous savings you can make by following the techniques in the book. Over time, you will find yourself returning to it again and again to look for new ways of making savings.

I am not promoting any specific service or products or providers, as different services / products and providers represent good value at different times and what's available in one city or region or country may not be available elsewhere. Instead, I have focused on savings tips that will be widely applicable.

What I am promoting is that you change your spending habits as outlined throughout this book. If you do so, you will reduce your outgoings and be in better control of your personal finances. I have tested the techniques outlined in this book over a number of years and have proved that they work. You'll see this in the **What I Did** sections in each chapter.

Reading this book and taking no action will result in you losing the cost of it. You must make an effort to tackle your expenses and to persevere until you make a saving with each one. The way to start is to make a list of all your bills and day-to-day spending and to work out how much you are spending in each area. Then tackle one expense at a time and record how much you are saving. Even after only a few months, you should be happily surprised at how much less you are spending.

What I Did

It is said that necessity is the mother of invention. I was inspired to start developing and using the techniques described in this book when the recession took hold and, as a family, we had less money coming in each month due to a combination of pay cuts and rising taxes. We weren't on the bread line but I was determined to spend smarter with the goal of reducing our spending by the same amount as the reduction in our household income – but I didn't want to make any significant lifestyle changes either. I liked the lifestyle we had.

I tried out these techniques over a few years and found that they worked. I spread the word to many friends and colleagues who told me that I should write them down and help other people – hence this book.

I have been using these techniques for over three years now and have proven that they work. I have saved over €5,000 a year as a result (€6,741 to be precise), with cumulative savings of over €15,000. Where else would I have got an extra €15,000 in after-tax income over the past three years? You can see how my savings built up in **Chapter 11: Principles & Practice**.

Your Next Steps

Read this book, from cover to cover, or dipping in and out at the sections that interest you or where you think you can make the most immediate savings.

Then register at **www.HowToSave5000.com** for more information to help you to manage your savings on an ongoing basis. And **you can save more than double the cost of this book immediately by signing up for the HowToSave5000 online course** – and then go on to save hundreds of times more using my constantly updated tips and techniques.

Good luck!

James O'Donovan
November 2012

2: Housing

My Annual Savings: €1,000+

Buying a House

The single biggest purchase that you are likely to make during your lifetime is a property to live in. Your decision will be based on a few main factors – location, price and size.

Location will affect the future value of your property, so a lot of thought needs to be put into that decision. Properties in good locations hold their value better and are easier to sell. Think long-term also, as moving house is expensive down the line with costs involved in both the selling and buying processes. Thinking long-term in terms of the location of your house also can yield savings in transport costs – for example, if your house is situated near a school, shops, public transport, etc., you will not need to spend money on transport costs to do school runs, go shopping, etc. These costs potentially accumulate over the years into thousands of euro.

Price and size are obvious factors. Don't buy a house you can't afford to pay for in the long-term. However, if you are buying a house that is well within your budget, bear in mind whether it will be suitable for the long-term if you should start a family and need more space. Paying a bit extra now for some extra room might save you money in the long term if you don't have to move to a bigger house. Another option is to buy a house with future potential and space around it to extend the living area. This means you don't have to spend money extending until you need to, so it's the best of both worlds.

Another factor, which often doesn't come into the decision process, is the cost of running and maintaining the house. Once you buy your house, you will want to have as few bills as possible so buying one with a good energy rating and insulation will result in significant energy (and thus financial) savings over the years. A house with a cost-effective heating system will have cheaper running costs. The aspect of the house also can help with energy savings – for example, if the living area of the house is south-facing, it will be warmer during the day and will need less energy to heat during daylight hours in the winter. It may be worth paying more for a house that is cheaper to run. However, this can reach a point where it could take many years to return the extra money spent on an energy-efficient house, so be sensible.

Mortgage

It can be difficult to get completely independent advice on which mortgage provider is best for you. You will find several websites showing the current mortgage interest rates of the different banks. The rates also are published in daily newspapers, so you will quickly see which institutions to avoid. The difference in how much you will end up paying over the lifetime of a mortgage could vary by tens of thousands of euro because of a tiny difference in the interest rate, so investing a lot of time in this research is vital.

Fixed Rate

The main choice you will have to make is whether you go for a fixed or variable rate. Put simply, with a fixed rate mortgage, the interest rate is set for an agreed period and you know exactly how much you will need to budget for each month. This may be suitable if you find it difficult to budget without knowing how much you are spending each month.

The advantage of a fixed rate mortgage is that if interest rates rise over the course of the fixed term, you will not be affected by the higher rates.

The downside is you may have to pay a penalty if you ever break the fixed term – for example, by moving house or moving to a cheaper mortgage provider. And, if interest rates drop over the course of the fixed term, you will not benefit from the lower rates.

Once you reach the end of the fixed term, the mortgage generally reverts to the standard variable rate, or you may have the option of fixing again for another period. This decision will be influenced by the rates available at the time.

Variable Rate

Variable rate mortgages will make your monthly budgeting a little more uncertain as you are not guaranteed to be paying the same amount each month. The rate – and thus your mortgage payment – can go up or down at the discretion of the financial institution. These types of mortgage are more suited to natural risk-takers.

The upside is that you have the advantage that you are free to switch to a cheaper mortgage provider at any time without any penalties. You also can change to a fixed term at any stage.

The downside is that the bank can raise the interest rate at its discretion and you are more exposed to general banking market conditions.

What's Best for You?

Which type of mortgage is best for you depends on whether you prefer the security of knowing how much your mortgage will be every month for a set number of years with a fixed rate mortgage, or whether you are happy with the chance that your monthly payments may rise, as well as fall, but that you incur no penalties for switching, in which case a variable rate mortgage is the one to go for.

If you are getting a new mortgage, regardless of the type, shop around relentlessly to get the lowest rate possible as there are considerable differences among what is on offer. Once you have secured a competitive mortgage, I recommend that you look at all available mortgage rates annually and see whether you can get a cheaper mortgage elsewhere (this applies mainly if you are on a variable rate). You need to factor in the costs of switching also, unless you manage to get the new financial institution to absorb the costs. Obviously, you will need some positive equity in your property – that is, the current market value of your property must be more than the current outstanding balance of the mortgage in order to switch.

Always check the terms and conditions before you sign up to any type of mortgage, or before you want to make a change to it.

Equity – Positive & Negative

Equity is the difference between the current balance of your mortgage and the current market valuation of your property. You have positive equity if your house is worth more than the current mortgage balance. You are in negative equity if the value of your house is less than the current balance of your house – for example, if your mortgage balance is €250,000 and the house is valued at €200,000, then you are €50,000 in negative equity. This does not impact you unless you are looking to sell your property, to move to a different property or to switch mortgage providers, in which case it will make all three scenarios difficult. If you are not doing any of the above, then it is irrelevant and the important point is to continue to make your payments.

Simple Tips for Paying Off Your Mortgage Sooner

Find out immediately what your current mortgage interest rate is by phoning your financial institution. Then stay up-to-date with mortgage interest rates, as outlined earlier, so you can pounce on a cheaper mortgage if it becomes available. The amount this one change can yield in savings cannot be overestimated. You could have the cost of this book covered in just a few days by doing so!

If you have extra money available, use it to pay off part of your mortgage, particularly during the early years where the interest is highest. This can be done by increasing the monthly payments by a fixed amount, or by depositing lump sums into your mortgage account. If you switch your mortgage payments to every two weeks, as opposed to the usual monthly payment, you also will make significant mortgage interest savings due to the fact you are making payments earlier each month and allowing less interest to accumulate as a result. Check with your lender whether any fees apply first before changing any terms of your mortgage like this.

Also investigate whether you would get a better return by putting your extra money in a savings account with a higher interest rate than your mortgage interest rate – if so, then money is better put into that account until such time as your mortgage interest rate is more than the deposit interest rate – for example, putting money on deposit at 3% is better than putting a lump sum into your mortgage when the mortgage rate is 2.5%.

What I Did

When tracker rates were still available, I switched my mortgage from standard variable to a tracker rate with a different institution.

Since then, the tracker rate has always been considerably lower than the standard variable equivalent, and in the first year it saved me about €1,000. Because this rate has been cheaper than either the fixed or variable equivalent over the past five years, that one simple move has saved me €5,000 over the period.

It is more difficult to switch mortgages these days, and trackers are no longer available, but the time will come where switching is an option, so be ready to move to a cheaper mortgage / institution when that time comes to save yourself some money.

Annual Savings: €1,000+

Rent

If you are renting a property or looking for a rented property, then the savings to be made come down to your ability to bargain. You need to get the best, most suitable rental accommodation for the least amount of rent.

The best approach is to research all rents in the area where you are planning to live and then get into discussions with the landlords of a few suitable properties. Renting a property outright on your own is more expensive than sharing with others. Typically, the more people you share with, the cheaper the rent – for example, two people renting a 2-bed property typically pay more rent each than three people renting a 3-bed property.

When you are looking for accommodation, you will notice some rentals are managed by agents and some are managed by the actual owner of the property themselves. It can be difficult to negotiate on the rent with agents as the decision is not theirs, and they need to look out for their commission. Dealing directly with the property owner can result in a better deal for you.

The main tips for negotiating cheaper rent with either the landlord or agent are as follows:

- If you have noticed that the property has been for rent for some time, then mention this and suggest that you would take it immediately if the rent was a little less.

- Have a detailed look at the property (don't walk in and say, "Wow this place is fabulous" – even if it is). Take note of anything that needs repair or is in bad condition – these can be used to negotiate.

- If you are a non-smoker, mention this; it will go in your favour most of the time.

- Do not sign up for longer than you need. The longest lease you should consider is 12 months. However, if you plan to stay there for several years, mention this to the landlord / agent as it could be another negotiating tool.

- Ensure you understand the lease terms and are aware of all costs that you will have to bear – for example, are electricity, heat and refuse collection costs yours or the landlord's responsibility?

- Also bear in mind the energy rating of the property, as this could lead to cheaper heating and electricity bills.

3: Utilities

My Annual Savings: €1,144

Electricity

There are several ways to reduce the cost of your electricity bill, as outlined below. As with a lot of the suggestions in this book, once you adopt these changes for a while they will become habitual and you will do them without thinking. It's said that you have to do something new seven times in order for it to become a habit.

To reduce your electricity bill:

- Change to a cheaper provider. Look online and watch out for TV and newspaper advertisements for alternative providers; then give them a call and make the switch. As with all service providers, check the fine print – look for minimum contract duration or penalties for breaking the contract. Switching to a cheaper provider usually can be done in minutes over the phone or internet – in most cases, you just need your current meter reading, meter identifier and

account number (on your last bill), and your direct
debit details. If you select direct debit as the payment
method and electronic billing instead of paper billing,
you may get additional discounts. Set a reminder in
your phone or calendar for the date the new contract
expires as you will be switched from the discount rate
to the normal rate then, and it will be time to shop
around again.

- When buying any electrical appliances, ensure you
  buy the one with the best energy rating possible. Also
  get an appliance suitable for your needs – don't get a
  bigger TV, bigger refrigerator, washing machine, etc.
  than you need. The bigger the appliance, the more
  electricity typically it uses.

- Make an inventory of everything in your house that
  uses electricity and think about how you could reduce
  the amount of electricity it uses. For example, switch
  all light bulbs to energy-saving bulbs. You will need
  to make an inventory of all bulbs in the house – the
  type of bulb, its wattage and whether it is on a
  dimmer switch. Bring this list to the shop with you, or
  buy the bulbs online. If you are confused about the
  different types of bulbs – for example, CFL *versus*
  halogen – then bring some of your existing bulbs to
  the shop with you and ask an assistant to suggest the
  correct energy-efficient replacements. Doing this
  throughout your house typically reduces your
  lighting costs by between 20% and 80%. If you want

to do this gradually, to avoid a big upfront cost, then start with the bulbs that are strongest and those that are turned on for the longest amount of time each day. There will be an initial financial outlay for this but it will result in significant savings long-term.

- Consider getting night-rate electricity. This can make financial sense if you only use your dishwasher, washing machine or tumble dryer at off-peak hours. Everything else that is powered on at night-time automatically will be cheaper also – for example, outdoor security lighting, alarm, refrigerator, etc. (or any of those other appliances that you accidentally left on standby overnight!). Details can be obtained from your electricity service provider. If your appliances – washing machine, tumble dryer, etc. – don't have built-in timers to start them at a certain time, then timers can be bought and plugged into the wall-socket and the appliance then plugged into the timers. For example, if your night rate electricity starts at midnight and you want to run the tumble dryer for 90 minutes, then set the timer to come on from 12:15 a.m. to 1:45 a.m. Or set it to start later, so your clothes can be still warm in the morning before you wear them – a nice treat at the start of the day!

- Switch off lights in a room when you leave it, unless you are going back into the room within a few minutes. Switch off all lights in the house before you leave, apart from any security lights. This will become a habit over time.

- Consider installing dimmer switches in some rooms – for example, the dining room or living / family rooms (check first that the bulbs in that room are suitable for use with a dimmer switch). Turning down the brightness of bulbs in these rooms when not reading etc. can create a nice atmosphere in the room – and uses less electricity.

- Don't leave appliances on standby overnight or when out of the house – for example, your TV, computer, audio / hifi, dishwasher, etc. Some electrical appliances can use a significant amount of electricity while on standby, as often there are other components using power apart from the little red LED indicator on the appliance.

- If you have a lot of empty space in your fridge or freezer, putting balloons or inflated and knotted plastic bags in these spaces will reduce the power usage of the fridge or freezer. Do not leave the door open for longer than needed.

- When using the oven, only pre-heat it a few minutes before you need to use it. If you are cooking or heating something small in the oven, consider using the microwave instead, which can be cheaper for small quantities of food.

- When boiling a kettle of water, only put in as much water as you need – for example, if you are making

just one cup of coffee for yourself, then just fill the
kettle to the minimum position.

- Electric tumble dryers can be very heavy on electricity
  and condenser dryers typically use more electricity
  than vented dryers. Consider drying your clothes
  outdoors when possible, or drying them on clothes
  horses indoors. If you do have to use the tumble
  dryer, they work more efficiently if items of a similar
  size are put in together because everything will only
  be dry as soon as the biggest and wettest item of
  clothing is dry. If you are purchasing a new dryer,
  look out for a dryer with good energy ratings, A is
  best, these will usually have a moisture sensor that
  turns it off automatically when the clothes are dry and
  they use half the energy of a C rated dryer through
  the use of Heat Pump technology.

- Wash clothes at a lower temperature where possible –
  for example, at 30°C instead of 40°C. Use the highest
  spin available for the clothes type – so the clothes will
  dry more quickly afterwards.

If your heating system is electricity-based, then consider
these tips for reducing your heating bill:

- Improve the insulation in your house, starting with
  the attic and then the walls.

- Draught-proof all doors and windows, but for safety
  ensure the house still has some ventilation.

- Use thermostats and timers where possible.

- Do not leave the heating on if you are on holidays for a week or more.
- Consider reducing the temperature. Savings of up to 10% can be made for every degree Celsius by which the temperature is reduced.
- Close the doors in rooms you are not using. Consider turning off the heating in those rooms also, or turning it down very low.
- If you have an open fireplace, consider putting a chimney balloon in place (it only takes two minutes) on winter evenings when a fire is not being lit. This stops the warm air in your house being sucked up the chimney – and cold air sucked in from the outside to replace it.

What I Did

Over the past few years, I have switched my electricity every year to get the cheapest provider. In general, this has saved me around 10% each year, or about €100 per year.

I switched all the light bulbs in my house to low energy CFL bulbs also – this reduced our lighting bill by 80%, amounting to a saving of approximately €200 per year. I also have installed a chimney balloon and draught-proofed all windows.

Annual Savings: €300

Note: I made an investment in light bulbs, a chimney balloon and draught-proofing but this cost will be returned in a few years – and should I sell my house these changes have made it more saleable.

Water

If you do not pay for water for domestic use, or you pay a set rate annually for it, then there is nothing you can do to about this cost.

However, if your water is metered and you pay more if you use more, then there are lots of ways to reduce this bill:

- Do not use more water than needed when cooking or boiling water in a kettle.

- Do not stay in the shower for longer than needed or leave taps running for longer than needed. Consider getting auto-shut off taps fitted.

- Use showers instead of baths whenever possible.

- Consider dual-flushing toilets with two buttons: one for a full flush, one for a partial flush.

- When your washing machine and dishwasher need to be replaced, buy water-efficient models.

- Buy a water butt, or look at rainwater harvesting systems. This water can be used for gardening, washing the car, or washing anything outdoors.

- Check whether you have any leaks – for example, underground. Do this by taking note of the meter reading if you are going on holidays for a week and checking it when you get back. Small differences can be accounted for by the fact the system may have been re-filling if you used water just before you left the house – for example, toilet or shower, or the freezer may have been making ice, etc. However, if there is a significant difference in the readings, then you may have a leak you didn't know about, which is costing you money.

Gas

The tips for reducing your gas bill are similar to those above for reducing your heating bill if electricity is your heating system.

Consider the cost benefits of upgrading to a high efficiency gas boiler – for example, a condensing boiler. These boilers use less energy, resulting in immediate savings.

As with electricity, switching to an alternative gas provider can yield significant savings immediately.

Make sure your boiler is serviced annually to ensure it is running efficiently – this is very important from a safety point of view but it also can reduce your gas bill.

What I Did

As with electricity, I switch to a different provider each year, saving about 10% or €150 per year.

We also service our boiler annually and have installed heating controls that divide the house into zones for more efficient heating. I bleed all radiators every few months and balance all radiators once a year. We put heat deflectors behind all radiators located on the external walls of the house. We upgraded the attic insulation and pumped insulation into the walls.

I noticed my annual gas bill drop by €250 from then on, accounted for by a combination of these measures.

Changing service provider: €150
Insulation and other techniques: €250
Annual Savings: €400

Note: I made an investment in insulation, zoned heating, radiator deflectors, etc. but this cost will be returned in a few years – and should I sell my house, these changes have made it more saleable.

Telephones / Broadband

There was a time when most, though not all, houses had a landline and mobile phones and broadband were not that common. There was not a lot of competition in the communications market at that time either, so the only way to reduce your phone bill was to make fewer calls. Now when most houses have a landline, broadband and several mobile phones, the total costs in this area are worth looking at.

Telephone / Broadband

Look at alternative providers for your landline, broadband, and mobile phones. More often than not, this will lead to instant savings. Look online – there are some great cost comparison websites that will select the cheapest provider for you. To get the best deal, you need to know your current usage, so these websites can calculate the best package to suit your needs – look over your recent bills for

the information you need to do this. You may end up with
landline, broadband and mobile phones all with the same
service provider or from different providers – whatever
permutation is cheapest.

Landline

Do you still need a landline for phone calls at home?
Monitor your phone calls for the next month to see how
often you are using it for making phone calls. Do not record
the incoming calls: these people would call you on your
mobile if you do not have a landline.

If you are using your landline for internet connectivity –
for example, for broadband – then look at alternative ways
of getting on the internet – for example, mobile or satellite
broadband or bundled with your cable TV (see later). You
may discover it no longer pays you to have a dedicated
landline.

But before you change, if you have a monitored alarm in
your house, check that this still can work without a landline
present.

If you have broadband, you can phone people using one
of several web-based VOIP (Voice Over Internet Protocol)
technologies. These calls are free once you are online! There
are several apps available on smartphones for free
phonecalls. Research the various options available.

Mobile

The simplest way to reduce mobile phone costs is to make
fewer calls and shorter calls. Send text messages unless you

really need to speak to the person. Only consider a longer conversation if you have free credit.

Other tips for reducing mobile phone bills include:

- If you are paying by the month, have a look at other packages available. You may be better off paying in advance. Examine your last month's bill and analyse other packages to see whether there are better options.

- Answer the call. Set your phone to ring for 30 seconds before it gets diverted to voicemail – if this is not an option on the phone, then contact your service provider online. A lot of phones are set to go to voicemail after 15 seconds, so you miss the call and have to phone the caller back. This costs the caller money (who may have paid for the time it took to leave a voicemail) and costs you money as you may have to phone them back – so the service provider is getting paid on the double.

- Try and spend a few days without using your mobile (but still keep it with you for emergencies obviously). It will feel very unusual at first but it might make you realise that you can survive without constantly texting, getting texts, checking if you got a text, checking for missed calls, etc. You also will spend less on those days you don't use the phone. Think about how you behave when it is running low on credit – try to use it this way all the time and your bill will reduce dramatically.

- Don't be tempted to change or upgrade your mobile phone too often unless it is free or the offer really benefits you. If your existing phone is problem-free, then don't change.

Avoid being tempted to take out mobile phone insurance, which many mobile phone providers may try to sell you. If you think about the cost of insuring the average house worth €200,000 at approximately €350 per year, or even the cost of insuring a car worth €10,000 at approximately €250 per year, then the cost of insuring a mobile phone looks very expensive relative to the value of the phone.

Don't be afraid to switch to a different provider – there are often great introductory offers and, in most cases, you can keep your existing number. Even if you get tied into a one-year contract, you can switch the following year again and get a new introductory offer from another provider. These introductory offers can be great value and the mobile phone provider has calculated that a large percentage of people will not move from them for a few years – so they get their profit from you in year two onwards – by which time you will have shopped around again.

What I Did

We have one landline for telephone and broadband, and two mobile phones. Our house has a monitored alarm which uses the landline to call us if the alarm is activated.

I used cost comparison websites to research the best packages and I set up my own spreadsheet to calculate which was cheapest. We changed our landline provider and got a cheaper package for calls and broadband. We stayed with the same mobile provider but got more suitable and cheaper mobile packages and thus reduced our total bill by €300 per year.

It took a lot of research to calculate the best packages, but it was worth it.

Changing landline / broadband service provider: €120
More suitable mobile packages: €180
Annual Savings: €300

Heating Oil

The same tips listed for reducing your heating bill apply to heating oil. In general, oil is the most expensive form of fuel, so consider getting an alternative means of heating your property – for example, natural gas, wood burners, air source heat pumps, etc.

If none of these options make economic sense, then it might be worth keeping an eye on the price of home heating oil as it fluctuates a lot. If you are almost out of oil in winter time, then you have no choice but to buy some – however, if the price is high, consider getting half a tank rather than a full tank. If the price drops during the year, consider filling the tank – even in the summer time – to take advantage of the lower price.

As with every purchase, make several phonecalls to get the cheapest supplier.

Also consider upgrading to a high efficiency condensing oil boiler – these will use considerably less oil to heat your house, particularly if combined with thermostatic heating controls within the house.

An oil boiler should be serviced annually, or every second year at a minimum, as this will help keep it running as efficiently as it did when it was new.

Cable / Satellite TV

Investigate the packages on offer from all suppliers to get the best deal. Do this once a year to keep up to date with what's on offer.

Don't sign up for more channels than you actually require.

Consider some of the free-to-air systems on the market – you would be surprised at how many channels you can get for free, once you have made an initial outlay on the receiving equipment.

Be careful of special offers giving you free movies or free sports channels for a few months – if you do not cancel these on a particular date, you will be charged the full price for them the following month.

It is possible to combine cable / satellite TV services with broadband and telephone services so you may reduce your overall TV and communications bill at the same time.

What I Did

When I examined the package I was on, I discovered that new packages had been introduced since I signed up to this provider several years ago. I switched to a different package with slightly fewer channels, but I still have all the channels I used to watch.

Annual savings: €60

Refuse Collection

The cost of refuse collection depends upon whether you are on a fixed payment package, a pay-by-weight package or a bin tags package. However, the following tips can help reduce your bill in all cases:

- If you are living in a housing estate, consider using one bin between you and your neighbour – this will reduce your refuse bill by 50% instantly.

- If you use pay-by-weight, try to reduce the weight of your bin by recycling as much as possible or starting a compost heap in your garden.

- Consider changing to a bin-tags scheme where you only pay for the days your bin is actually collected.

- Shop around annually for a cheaper provider – often you will get a discount the first year – so by changing provider every year, you always get this discount.

- Phone your current provider and ask if they have any suggestions for reducing your bill.

- Consider having less refuse to begin with – for example, by throwing away less food or by buying fewer products that are over packaged.

What I Did

I phoned my current refuse collection provider to ask for suggestions on reducing my bill and I found out that if I used a smaller refuse bin it would save me €84 per year.

Annual savings: €84

4: Food

My Annual Savings: €2,331

Groceries

Your annual grocery bill is most likely your single biggest expense after rent or mortgage payments. It makes sense, therefore, to spend time coming up with strategies that will lead to big savings.

Here are some practical tips to help reduce this large bill:

- Don't buy more food than you need. Start looking at how much food you throw away after each meal or at the end of the week from the refrigerator. If you regularly throw away food at the end of a meal, then start cooking a little less food to begin with. Make a list of the food and groceries you throw away each week to help you decide which items you need to buy less of from now on – this is quite easy to do. There may be an added bonus of reducing the weight of your refuse bin and saving money there – it's one thing to pay for the food you buy but then not using the food and paying to dispose of it is money wasted on the double.

- Never shop for groceries when you are hungry. You'd be surprised how much unnecessary food you buy when your resistance is low due to hunger!

- For items with a reasonable shelf life, consider buying them in larger quantities – for example, a 1kg bag of pasta instead of a 500g bag. Groceries, more often than not, are cheaper when bought in larger quantities. A lot of supermarkets display the price per kg, or per litre, which will help you find the best value. In general, the bigger size you buy, the cheaper it is per unit.

- When buying perishable items – for example, fruit, vegetables, milk – always check the best-before date, otherwise you may have to throw it away before you have used all of it because it has gone out of date. If the best-before date has expired, or is too close, then try and find one with a later date.

- For non-perishable items – for example, cosmetics or cleaning agents – buy in large containers always for best value, and if there is a special offer (2 for the price of 1), then stock up and buy 10 or 12 of them, even if this is 12 months' supply. These items can be stored in your house for months, years even, and you have made a considerable saving.

- Most supermarkets have an online shopping website and all the current offers will be posted there. Look at the supermarket's website before you go shopping so you are aware of all offers.

- Consider buying some cheaper brands of food from time to time or doing some of your shopping in lower cost supermarkets. Compare the price of different brands of the same product in the shop – particularly the supermarket's 'own brand' – and you will see big differences in the prices. Although some of the brands on sale in the low cost supermarkets may not be familiar to you, it is worth trying them out and enjoying the savings in the process. You may end up splitting your weekly shopping over more than one supermarket or shop if you have time and if it pays you to do so, or you can split your weekly shopping between your partner and yourself, one doing the cheaper supermarket and the other doing the usual supermarket. It can be worth the extra effort to make the additional savings. It is also worth noting that supermarkets often place the most profitable items at eye-level so look to the top and bottom of the shelves where cheaper brands might be displayed.

- Plan your weekly shopping wisely. Try to avoid having to return to smaller convenience stores during the week as they are a lot more expensive and it increases the temptation to buy something you don't need.

- Making home-cooked meals instead of buying readymade meals is much healthier and also a lot cheaper. Invest in one or two good cookbooks and see how little a good meal can cost while also learning a new skill.

- Learn how to make homemade soups, pizzas, simple pasta dishes or quiches as these can be a good simple way of using 'left-over' vegetables at the end of the week and having a healthy meal in the process.

- Make the most of vouchers or the points / rewards systems your regular supermarket might have. Ensure both you and your partner get a card for the same rewards account, so any time one of you gets something then all points are going to the same account for maximum benefit.

What I Did

First, I put a lot of effort into this area as it is our second biggest annual bill after our mortgage, and I continue to work on new savings in this area each month.

I check all offers on the supermarket website before I go shopping and I always try to capitalise on these offers – for example, if dishwasher tablets are half-price, I will buy a year's supply; if there is 50% extra free on an item, I will try to buy this if we need it.

We split our shopping over one low cost supermarket (which I do) and one regular supermarket (which my wife does). Right now, about 20% of our weekly shop is in the low cost supermarket.

We both check the best-before and use-by dates to make sure we don't buy anything that will expire before we use it.

We signed up for the rewards systems in both supermarkets.

It is difficult to calculate the precise total annual savings but I have been recording the savings made as I switch from one item to a cheaper item. It might seem trivial and cumbersome doing this one item at a time but that is the best way to see exactly what you are saving – for example:

- Oranges: we have freshly-squeezed orange juice each morning and I was surprised at how much this had been costing. I found very good quality oranges in a local low cost supermarket and we now spend €306.60 less per year on our freshly-squeezed orange juice.

- Milk: we use 3 litres of skimmed milk and 2 litres of regular milk every week – this had been costing us €1.23 per litre for skimmed and €1.08 per litre for regular. I now buy these in a local low-cost supermarket for €0.85 and €0.75 respectively. Our annual milk bill now costs us €93.60 less per year.

- Tinned tomatoes: we use approximately two tins per week and had been paying €0.99 per tin for a well-known brand. We switched to one of the supermarkets' 'own brands', which costs €0.50 per tin – this saves us €50.96 per year.

These three simple changes save us €451.16 annually. I have tabulated lots of other grocery savings and the total annual savings amounts to approximately €1,250 per year – and I am still making more savings each month as I am constantly working on this.

I can see myself saving over €2,000 on our annual grocery bill by the time I am finished working on this bill, but it is one that I will probably never be finished with.

Annual Savings: €1,250

Food at Work / Snacks

Food bought outside of the main weekly grocery shopping can be costing a lot more than you think, as it is bought in small amounts, and often in convenience stores or petrol stations, and doesn't seem like a large annual cost unless all these small purchases are added together – for example, a take-away coffee and / or scone a few mornings a week, the occasional lunch in a café or bar, over-priced pre-packed sandwiches, etc.

There are a considerable number of people also who, when they enter a shop to buy a take-away coffee or sandwich, also buy something they don't really need – for example, a magazine, lottery tickets, sweets / confectionary, or gadgets for sale usually located near the cash register. If you made a list of how much you spend on this over a few weeks, I think you might be surprised.

Here are a few simple tips to reduce this hidden, but expensive, habit:

- If you like a coffee in the morning, buy a carry-out mug, and fill it with coffee before you leave the house. This will save you a considerable amount of money each year. It also will save you time spent parking and then queuing in the shop, and will prevent you from being tempted to buy other non-essential items whilst in the shop. It will help the environment as you will be reducing the manufacture and disposal of potentially hundreds of disposable coffee cups each year – and you also get to drink your favourite coffee.

- Consider bringing your lunch with you to work. This involves making sandwiches at home, which also may improve your diet as you are in control of what you put in your sandwiches (for example, the amount of butter, low fat spreads, salt, etc.). Alternatively, consider cooking a little extra food for dinner the night before (or better again, instead of throwing away the excess food you cooked and were going to dump), place it in the fridge overnight and bring it to work the following day where it can be reheated. If you are partial to an afternoon snackbar, buy them in multipacks at the supermarket instead of paying too much for them in vending machines at work.

What I did

My wife had been buying a coffee on the way to work each morning for €2. This cost €10 per week or approximately €460 per year. She bought a coffee mug for €10 and a bag of Fairtrade coffee for €2.99 which makes about 15 large mugs of coffee. This has saved us €9 per week or over €414 per year.

For several years, I had been buying a scone at work for a morning tea break (€1.40) and buying lunch in a subsidised canteen (€3.90), costing €26.50 per week or €1,219 annually. Then I decided to make my own sandwiches in the morning before going to work and also bring bread and butter to work to make toast for the morning tea break. This costs approximately €12 per week and saves me approximately €667 per year.

It's hard to imagine that you can have €1,081 extra in your pocket in a year by making these two changes, but it's true.

Annual Savings: €1,081

5: Children

My Annual Savings: €150

Rechargeable Batteries

When you have a child, you will find yourself buying lots of things you never bought previously during your weekly shopping – for example, baby food, clothes for a growing child, diapers/nappies, baby wipes – all the normal extra purchases you would expect when there are children in the household.

One purchase that doesn't immediately pop into your mind when children arrive is batteries. However, a lot of your children's toys will be battery-operated. It took me a while to realise how many batteries we had been buying. It was only when I saw how many we had collected for recycling that I began to think about how much we had spent on them. If a child becomes dependent on a particular toy or gadget for getting to sleep, etc. and you discover the batteries are flat, you will pay anything to get your hands on new batteries. And, over time, the cost of batteries to power toys and gadgets builds up.

Every week in the supermarket, I see families buying large packages of cheap brand batteries as part of their weekly shopping. These batteries will probably be used up before the weekend is out – particularly if the weather is bad and children need to spend more time inside playing with their toys. Rechargeable batteries are the answer!

First, you need a good battery charger. Don't skimp here. I went through several cheap battery chargers for different-sized batteries that took up to 8 hours to fully charge the batteries before I realised that I should have bought a top-of-the-range battery charger. The charger I use now charges the three most commonly-used battery sizes in 15 minutes from flat. Although expensive, it was one of the best purchases I have made in quite a while. It has worked a treat for the past five years and, when we go on holidays, it's near the top of our checklist – just after tickets and passports!

To summarise go for a top-of-the-range charger, with the shortest possible charge time, and the ability to take different battery sizes. The earlier you start this, the better.

Second, you need good quality rechargeable batteries. Like most people, I initially thought there was not much to this, just buy any rechargeable battery, preferably the cheapest. But I was wrong – the most important property of a rechargeable battery is how many mAH (milli-amp hours) it has. In simple terms, the higher the mAH figure, the longer the battery will last when fully charged – and as rechargeable batteries cannot be recharged forever, then the less often you have to recharge them, the more years you will get out of them. A device that uses 1000mAH of power per hour will last for one hour on fully-charged 1000mAH rechargeable batteries, but will last for 2.5 hours on fully-charged 2500mAH rechargeable batteries. So the mAH rating is important.

There is an initial outlay on a battery charger and rechargeable batteries (you will need several sets of batteries for the most commonly-used toys) are more expensive than ordinary batteries. Long term, however, rechargeable batteries work out significantly cheaper. Take an average toy that uses 4 AA batteries at an average cost of €3.50 for a medium-to-good brand. If you go through a set of these every two weeks (easily achievable), this could cost you €91 per year just on this one toy. Four rechargeable AA batteries, from a good brand, will cost approximately €18 and will last for at least 26 charges – so you can achieve a saving of €73 per year for each set of four batteries. If you have five toys on the go, using four batteries each, you can see how much you could save annually.

Note: some toys have a warning that they are not suitable for rechargeable batteries, so watch out for that and don't buy these toys!

Also there is a significant environmental benefit to using rechargeable batteries on an ongoing basis.

What I did

I bought a good brand battery charger that charges four batteries in 15 minutes and will take different sized batteries. I bought enough sets of good brand rechargeable batteries to cover four or five toys, these batteries had the highest mAH rating I could find.

I have not calculated exactly how much per year I have saved from this but it is easy to see, from above, that I have saved at least €150 per year with one child – and that's a conservative estimate.

Annual Savings: €150

Baby Food

Make your own baby food and save money. You also will be in full control of all ingredients. This takes a little more effort but, if it is done once a week and the daily meals are frozen in containers for each day of the week, then it reduces the extra effort. There are lots of suitable recipes online.

Nursery Equipment

Buying a full set of nursery equipment can be very expensive when you include a buggy, feeding chair, cot, etc. Some multi-terrain buggies can cost more than a high-end TV.

There are significant savings to be made from buying these items secondhand or from a relative. Lots of stores have opened up in recent years supplying these items secondhand. Some of these items may have been used only for one or two children, perhaps even for only a few months each, and have years of safe use left in them.

However, when it comes to car seats and booster seats, always buy new from a safety point of view.

6: Banking &
Personal Finance

My Annual Savings: €270

Fees & Interest

Stop paying bank fees, simple as that. Contact your bank
and find out the criteria for not paying fees. If there is not
an option, or you cannot meet the criteria, contact other
banks until you find one where you can avoid paying bank
fees.

Current Account

A current account typically pays no interest, or a very low
interest rate. Find out what the situation is with your
current account. Enquire from the bank whether you can
get interest on your current account. If not, the best thing is
to keep only the minimum amount of money you need in
this account – for example, for paying day-to-day bills, rent,
mortgage, etc.

Calculate what you need in the account each month and, if you are lucky enough to have extra money each month, then move it to a savings account with a higher interest rate. A lot of people leave a lot of money in their current account for years on end, earning little or no interest, when this money could be in a deposit account earning money for them.

Of course, it goes without saying that you save a lot of money by operating your current account in credit and not having an overdraft. Overdrafts are expensive – especially unauthorised overdrafts, where you slip into the red unintentionally. Keep an eye on your balance each week and make sure your accounts stays in credit.

Savings Account

In general, there are three common forms of saving account:

- On-demand: this is where you have instant access to your savings, sometimes on 24 hours' or 7 days' notice – several variations of on-demand savings account exist. At the very least, it is better than having money in your current account. However, it usually pays the lowest interest of all savings accounts in return for the convenience of instant access to your savings. The best approach is to put just enough money here to cover an emergency, and to move anything above that amount to one of the other savings accounts below.

- Regular savings account: this is a savings account that requires a certain amount to be saved each month (within lower and upper limits, but the monthly amount can be changed quite easily). The interest rate is generally quite good on these accounts and it encourages regular savings which is great. It is not suitable for lump sums as you can only transfer money into it monthly. Usually, withdrawals can be made at will but there might be some penalty – check the terms and conditions.

- Fixed term savings account: this is a savings account in which a lump sum can be deposited for a fixed term – for example, three months, one year, three years, etc. – the longer the term, the better the interest rate on these accounts. Withdrawals may not be allowed until the term is complete – check the terms and conditions – so it is important to be sure that you do not need the money within the term.

In summary, keep only the minimum amount of money in your current account, set up a combination of savings accounts that allows you to have some money on demand, and more of it locked away, but all of it earning more interest than the current account.

What I Did

I had been paying approximately €60 per quarter, or €240 per year, on bank fees. It was only when I started this whole project of trying to save €5,000 in a year that I realised bank fees would be free if I met certain conditions.

The conditions vary from bank to bank but, in my case, if I keep my current account balance above a specified minimum amount and make one online transaction per quarter, I pay no fees. I make sure I meet these criteria now and this saves me €60 every three months.

I also set up an on-demand savings account and a regular savings account. The interest I receive is not a lot, but I had been getting nothing for it while this money was in the current account.

Annual Savings: €240+

Credit Cards

Banks love credit cards. They charge up to 20%, or more, interest on the balance, yet they only pay you a few percent on your savings accounts, so there are clearly huge profit margins for the banks at your expense.

The best tips for a credit card are:

- Get rid of it. Can you use a debit card instead? Most online purchases and purchases over the phone can be made using debit cards nowadays. You'll also avoid paying the annual stamp duty (€30 currently) on credit cards, and you'll eliminate completely the chance of getting caught by credit card fraud as you no longer have a credit card – this alone has the potential to save you thousands.

- If you must have a credit card, then pay the full amount each month, or set up a direct debit whereby the full amount is paid each month – banks will do this if you persuade them, however they will not make a cent out of your credit card by doing so.

- Also, if you do need a credit card, just have one between you and your partner.

- If you feel you cannot pay off the balance on your credit card every month, shop around for a better credit card, with lower interest rates – sometimes 0% interest cards are available.

- If you have an existing bill on your credit card that you can never seem to get on top of, then try to get a personal loan to pay off the full balance. The interest rate on the personal loan will be substantially less than on the credit card.

What I Did

We had two credit cards and, although we used to pay the full balance each month, we sometimes missed the date by accident and paid a little interest. We switched the payment of both of these cards to direct debit whereby the full amount is paid each month. From that day on, we would never have to pay interest on the credit card again.

Shortly after that, I got rid of my credit card, which saves me €30 per year on stamp duty. I use my debit card for everything now.

Annual Savings: €30+

Loans

As with everything, shop around for the best possible rate. Also consider every option before you take out the loan. Could you put off the purchase for another year and save a bit more towards the cost of the item? It is always cheaper not to get a loan – always.

If the loan is to buy a car, then think about getting a slightly cheaper car and borrowing less, or better again borrowing nothing. If the loan is for house improvements, ensure you shop around for the best price for the job – perhaps you could do some of the work yourself and save money – for example, painting, fitting skirting boards, tiling – thus learning a new skill and saving money.

As with all financial transactions, check all terms and conditions. Bear in mind also that, if you run into difficulty paying off even a small loan, it will affect your credit rating, and this could make it more difficult or expensive to get a more important, bigger loan in the future.

What I did

I did nothing here as I did not have any loans at the time of writing this book, apart from my mortgage.

I got one car loan for my first car and, since then, I have not bought a car until I had the money saved for it – that was about six cars ago. The cost of running a car is already very expensive without the extra weight of a car loan.

7: Insurance

My Annual Savings: €686

For all insurance products, get quotations from at least three companies before you decide on an insurance company. I am amazed every year when I get my usual renewal letters offering "the best prices possible having extensively searched the markets etc, etc." and, within five minutes on the internet, I have found a cheaper quotation. This year when I switched, the company actually said, "Why didn't you tell us and we could have matched the price?", to which I responded, "Why didn't you offer that price in my renewal letter and I would not have switched to begin with?".

It is very important with all insurance to be 100% honest. If you lie when getting a quotation, then chances are you will not be covered in the event of a claim and, even if your premium was only €1, then that €1 has been wasted. The first thing insurance companies do when you put in a claim is find out whether it's valid, and then check whether you have met all the terms and conditions.

Try to pay your insurance premiums up front. Do not opt for monthly direct debits unless this does not end up costing you more – if it is a 0% interest direct debit, then go ahead with it.

Car

My tips for getting cheaper car insurance are:

- Obviously, shop around each and every year until you find the cheapest deal. Very often, insurance brokers have an administration fee of €25 to €50 that they can play with. Ask if they can waive that fee or part of it.

- Increase the 'excess' on the policy – the amount you have to pay yourself in a claim – for example, if you claim €1,000 and your excess is €200, then you must pay the first €200. The higher your excess, the lower your premium, so enquire if your premium would be less if you had a higher excess. If not, then make your excess as low as possible.

- Consider cheaper cover, bearing in mind it is cheaper for a reason but, if you want to reduce your costs, you may have to consider this option. For example, comprehensive cover is the most expensive and, if your car is relatively new, then it is advisable to have this cover so you will get the open market value of your car if it is written off. However, if your car is only worth up to €1,000, then it is not worth getting comprehensive cover. Third party fire and theft is cheaper and will do in that case. If your car is worth less again (only a few hundred euro) then third party cover, which is the cheapest and minimum available, will do.

- Enquire whether adding your partner as a named driver will reduce the premium, often it does.

- If you drive very little – perhaps only 5,000 miles per year – there are often discounts available, so enquire.

- Drive safely and try not to have an accident! If you have five years or more claims-free driving, there is a significant reduction in your premium (usually 50%+). If you have a claim, this can be wiped out (unless you opted in to protect your no-claims bonus – which again costs extra). So try not to have any claims as the cost is not just the cost of a new car, but substantially higher insurance premiums for another five years to get back your full no claims bonus.

- Reduce the chances of a claim also by parking in safe well-lit areas and leaving nothing exposed in your car. This reduces the risk of you having to claim for theft or damage.

What I Did

I have paid approximately the same price for car insurance the past few years, but each time the premium on my renewal letter was up to €100 more than what I ended up paying. So each year, I apply the tips above and get covered for the same as the previous year, or less – so I save €100 per year compared to the renewal offer.

Annual savings: €100

House

Your house is your most valuable asset (even if the bank really owns it). As with all insurance, honesty is vital. In fact, house insurance is quite good value considering it can be cheaper than car insurance at times yet your house is worth substantially more than your car.

However, there are savings to be made with house insurance also as follows:

- Research your building costs annually. A lot of people are over-insured. In the current recession, building costs have come down substantially so it will cost less to rebuild your house now. As a result, your house insurance premium should reflect that. Check it out before you start shopping around for insurance prices.

- Similar to car insurance, increase the excess only if it reduces the premium. Having a higher excess in a house insurance policy is not as risky as in a car, as a serious house insurance claim will be in the order of tens of thousands of euro, or more, so an excess of €1,000 won't be that high, relatively speaking.

- House insurance is cheaper if you can get all the discounts so make sure you have the recommended smoke alarms, security locks on doors / windows, monitored house alarm, etc. Beware of the fine print though – I have seen conditions as follows: "security locks on all downstairs windows must be locked when you leave the house. The alarm must always be set when leaving the house". Again, read the fine print and comply with it, or your insurance is worth nothing.

What I Did

House insurance has gone up a lot in the past few years and, when my renewal letter came in last year at over €100 more compared with the previous year, I applied the tips above to reduce it.

I first investigated my rebuilding costs using a reputable website; this reduced my building costs. I also increased my excess to €1,000, then I shopped around online with five companies and finally got a satisfactory quotation €103 cheaper than that quoted in my renewal letter.

Annual Savings: €103

Life

The way to cheaper life insurance is quite straightforward in principle, but not in practice. Give up smoking if you smoke, and either do not drink alcohol or don't drink more than the limits shown on your policy. The healthier you are, the cheaper the insurance – simple. Age comes into it also but this is beyond your control, unfortunately.

Outside of this, simply shop around for the best price and look for discounts for new customers. Always check the fine print with a policy to ensure you have continuity of cover when switching from one provider to another.

Mortgage protection

If you have mortgage protection, which is required by most banks, then there are some techniques to make this cheaper, in addition to the tips for getting cheaper life insurance as outlined in the previous section above.

Look out for companies offering discounts for the first year – for example, discounts of up to 70% are available in year one, with no obligation to stay for a second year. Most people do not switch after year one, but I have switched every year, so I have been getting a reduction every year.

Each year, the balance of your mortgage decreases and obviously the term is one year closer to the end. So if you switch (which you should), then you need to cover only the term *remaining* and the balance *remaining* (not the *original* term and amount), so instead of still paying mortgage protection on a 25-year mortgage of €300,000, you should possibly be getting cover for a 21-year mortgage with a balance of €250,000, which is cheaper.

What I Did

I had been paying an average of €680 per year on a mortgage protection policy.

I shopped around a few years ago and discovered discounts of up to 70% on year one for a new customer, with no obligation to renew with the company in year two.

My premium went down from €680 to approximately €272 (based on 60% discount). I did that each year since then and effectively have been paying 60% less for mortgage protection insurance ever since. I also update the term remaining and the outstanding balance on the new policy each year to ensure I am not over-insured.

Annual Savings: €408

Travel

Travel insurance is optional. However, most people tag it onto the package holiday they are buying or buy it when they are buying their plane tickets online – but that is not the cheapest way to do it.

There are several companies online where you can buy annual multi-trip travel insurance. This often can cost the same annually as it would be to buy once when tagged onto a package holiday or through the airline's website.

By buying annual multi-trip travel insurance from a separate online insurance company, you will be covered for several trips abroad – for example, if you are lucky enough to take more than one holiday per year, or even a city break over a weekend, you are still covered.

The usual advice of shopping around online and comparing the actual benefits applies.

Additional discounts may be available if you have private health insurance that covers you for medical cover abroad.

What I did

Between a sun holiday, short city break and a trip or two abroad for work each year, I took out annual multi-trip travel insurance which gives me the benefit of having peace of mind on holidays as well as saving approximately €75+ per year if I bought insurance separately with each trip.

Annual Savings: €75

8: Personal &
Household

My Annual Savings: €260

Personal and household bills can amount to smaller figures compared with insurance, etc. but there is still significant room for savings.

Sell Off Old Items

When it comes to furniture, fittings, appliances, TVs, garden tools, lights, etc., if they are broken beyond repair, then there is no choice but to replace them. However, a lot of these purchases are because you want a newer TV, a change in sofa as you think the old one is tired or you want to give a room a makeover and get new lights, curtain rails, etc.

Don't forget that one man's rubbish is another man's treasure. If a sofa, TV, light, curtain rail, lawnmower, etc. is in reasonable working order, then it has a certain monetary value and can be sold. There are numerous free or cheap ads on newspapers and online websites dealing in this. It makes financial sense to sell the old item as it gives some money to go toward your new purchase and you also avoid the potential cost of disposing of the old item. Further, it makes environmental sense as your old item is going to a new home instead of the local landfill site.

You would be amazed at how many people are out there searching these types of ads for second-hand furniture, electrical appliances, etc. for rental properties, student accommodation, or their own houses.

What I Did

The first time this idea came to my mind was when I was buying a new electric lawnmower mainly because I wanted a wider one that would cut the lawn more quickly. My existing electric lawnmower had been used a lot over the years. I had bought it for €100 in a sale, reduced from €150, and it was in perfect working order still. I was about to take it apart and dispose of it when I got the idea to try and sell it. I advertised it for €50 in a local free ads newspaper supplement and I was surprised at how many calls I got. I had it sold within a week and got €50 which I then put towards the new bigger electric lawnmower I bought (which I also bought in a sale).

While we are on the subject of lawnmowers, consider buying an electric lawnmower instead of a petrol one – they do not need to be serviced, do not run out of petrol and are very quiet and light (plus they always start first time). Get the strongest motor you can get, as the smaller wattage models are not strong enough for high grass. Also make note of the lead length and the collection box size, as these vary considerably.

After my successful lawnmower sale, I did the very same thing, or tried it at least, every time I was making a similar purchase. Over the years, I have sold a three-piece suite of furniture, table and chairs, TV and coffee machine and used the money to go towards new purchases. This strategy works when upgrading something rather than replacing something that is broken.

Again, all the new purchases I made were at reduced sale prices. You will also get to meet some interesting people during these transactions and will develop your sales skills which are skills that can be used in a variety of situations.

Annual Savings: buying furniture, electrical appliances, etc. is not really an annual bill so I have not included it in the total savings – but it has certainly saved me money over the years.

Furniture

When buying new furniture, look out for sales, as there are often great discounts available.

Consider checking out some of the second-hand ads online or in a local paper – there are often almost-new items of furniture for sale at a fraction of the cost. Good furniture wears really well and a well-looked-after leather suite or solid wood dining table and chairs can be as good five years old as it was new, and you pay a substantially lower price for it.

Buy classic furniture where possible, so it will be easier for you to sell it down the line if you want a change. Avoid loud colours, artificial wood, faux leather, etc. There is always demand, for example, for a black leather suite. If you buy the jazzy white suite or lemon-coloured one, while it has the wow factor for now, it will be very difficult to sell in the future if you want to trade up to a new suite. It also will be difficult to keep clean.

Leather suites are a better investment than fabric suites, and sometimes they are the same price. They are much easier to sell down the line, easier to keep clean and wear better. Avoid falling for the expensive care warranties for spills, etc. but, to be on the safe side, do some research on what to do if you spill wine or something like that on the leather so that you are prepared if it happens.

Kitchen / Electronic Appliances

Tips here include:

- Buy the most energy-efficient appliances you can afford – the energy rating will be displayed somewhere on the appliance – as it will save you money in the long run. There is no doubt that energy prices are only going to rise in the future.

- Do some research online to see the best brands. You will discover that some well-known brands also sell their products under cheaper brand names but the products are essentially the same 'under the skin' – so buying the cheaper of their brands will save you money but you still end up with a quality product.

- Checkout the warranties. Most appliances come with a one-year or three-year warranty which is sufficient. However, if you have to post off a signed form or complete a form online to activate the warranty, then do not forget to do this. Try not to get persuaded by the sales people into buying extended warranties – these often can be pricey and are not really that important if you are buying a good quality reliable product to begin with.

- Keep the manuals also. They will be invaluable down the line for troubleshooting a problem that you might otherwise think is the end of the appliance or that you might need to get a service callout to fix.

- Follow any routine maintenance mentioned in the manuals –for example, cleaning / replacing filters, etc. – as this will reduce the overall cost of ownership.

- Follow the installation instructions also as this can prolong the life of the appliance – for example, a washing machine should be perfectly balanced so that when it is spinning at 1200 rpm, there is minimal wear on the drives and belt – this will lead to it lasting longer.

- Watch out for end-of-season or end-of-line sales. Significant discounts can be had on the 'old model' washing machine for example, which is still quite likely a very good and energy-efficient appliance but lacking the fancy touch screen of the new model, or is in the 'old season' colour or something like that.

- Think long-term also. It might be worth buying that bigger capacity washing machine now, or the larger dishwasher – in the event your family expands and you realise your existing appliance is too small for your new needs.

- Only buy the appliances you really need or can afford – built-in coffee-makers, wine chillers, etc. are not essential, for example.

- Consider a washer / tumble dryer combined, which take up less space and usually are cheaper than buying a separate washing machine and dryer – however, ensure the energy rating is good as dryers can be very heavy on electricity.

- A tumble dryer comes in vented and condenser form – in general, the vented dryers are more efficient once you can vent them to the outside of the house. Some new dryers have moisture sensors so that they stop when the clothes are dry instead of continuing to operate for the preset period of time even though the clothes are dry.

Barber shop / Hairdressers

Hair continues to grow (as long as you still have it), so you have to get your hair cut from time to time.

For men, if your haircut involves the use of a scissors, then you cannot do it yourself so the only way to save money is find somewhere cheaper to get it cut, or get it cut a little less often. Most barbers or unisex hair salons charge less for a dry cut, so consider this instead of a wash, cut and blow-dry. Even at this, I have seen price differences of 30%

to 40% in the price for a dry cut in some standard barbers / unisex salons in my locality.

If your haircut involves only a shaver – for example, Number 2 or 4 or a skinhead – then you can do this yourself at home very easily by buying a shaver / trimmer. You will have it paid for in one year easily.

For women, the obvious saving is to shop around, as prices vary hugely for women's hairdressers. If you live outside a city and usually get your haircut in the city, then consider getting it done locally or in the suburbs, thus saving also on parking fees in the city for the many hours you may be at the hairdresser. Make a few phone calls to find out prices, try out some of these places and you will find somewhere that you are happy with but is less expensive.

If you dye your hair, then you could consider returning to your natural colour and saving on this cost, even if only for occasionally. There are also several dye kits you can buy and try out at home or with a friend at a fraction of the cost.

Alternatively, you may be able to find a hairdresser who will come to your house for less than it costs you normally to go to a hairdresser who is paying for premises.

What I Did

I used to get my hair cut regularly every four weeks and had been paying €15 for a dry cut. This was an area in which I thought I would not save money but I simply decided to get my hair cut every five weeks instead, and I shopped around and found a place nearby that charges €10 for a dry cut and the standard is perfect.

Again, this sounds like something that is not worth the trouble but my annual haircut bill went from €195 to approximately €100 to €110, so I almost halved this bill.

If you have children, then you could literally save almost €100 a head annually by doing this.

My wife had been in the habit of getting her hair cut in the city centre in an upmarket salon. This also involved typically two to three hours' multi-storey car parking fees. Having done a little research, she found a salon in the suburbs, with free parking, and got her hair done to the same standard for 30% less. For even just four visits per year, this amounts to €40 saved in car parking fees and about €120 saved in hairdressing fees.

Annual Savings: €260

Fitness

Staying fit and getting enough exercise is vital and has to be maintained. However, there are ways to do this while also saving money.

If you are a member of a health club or gym, enquire about group rates. These are usually available to companies in the corporate sector. However, very often, they will be offered to a group of individuals who come together, so if you could get five or 10 of your friends to come together, you may be able to negotiate a group discount.

Most health clubs and gyms are cheaper outside peak hours so maybe you could go early in the morning before work – you will be saving money, arrive at work energised and have the evening after work completely free.

26 Aug. 2021 2:20 PM

Train your brain to get rich : the simple
program that primes your gray cells for

Date Due: **16 Sep 2021**

How to save 5000 : this year and every
year : reduce your outgoings without

Date Due: **16 Sep 2021**

If you have space in your home, consider buying one item of professional gym equipment each year instead of joining the gym – for example, buy a cross-trainer, then a rowing machine, etc. Within five years, you will be well on your way to having your own gym at home and it will be free membership from then onwards. If you do decide to change back to the gym, then you will be able to recoup some money by selling the gym equipment and you will still have saved money overall.

Consider combining exercise with something you do everyday – for example, cycle to / from work, get the bus to work and run home (once your working day is finished …) – this way you get your workout as part of an already existing task to make the most of your time.

Consider running. This is the cheapest exercise as a small investment in decent running shoes and gear is all that is needed. It's also extremely versatile – you can do it anywhere and a 30-minute run a few times a week will keep anyone in great shape.

Toiletries

The simple trick of buying in bigger quantities is the easiest way to make savings here. Go for large volumes of shower gels or shampoos. Stock up when you see '2 for 1' offers or '20% extra free', etc. These products are non-perishable so buy large quantities when they are cheap. Experiment with some cheaper brands also.

When it comes to men's shaving, the cost of top-end disposable razor blades has become quite high and some of the high-tech electric razors cost as much as a basic TV these days. If you are determined to make a simple saving here, then consider cheaper brands of shaving gel – and consider switching brands of razor.

The savings from the next tip would take years to save even €1, but to get you out of a fix next time you run out of shaving gel during a shave – simply place the container under a hot tap for 20 to 30 seconds and then try again – you will get enough gel / foam out for another shave. The reason for this is these containers are designed to run out of air pressure before they run out of gel / foam, so heating it under a tap increases the air pressure and uses the remaining gel and foam. There is a minimal saving financially, but it can be extremely valuable if you run out of shaving gel / foam on the morning of a job interview, for instance.

Books & Magazines

As you have already bought this book, then I shouldn't criticise you for buying new books. However, second-hand books are readily available and very cheap.

Joining a local library is a great way to have instant access to thousands of books for a fraction of the cost of buying.

Consider e-books as an alternative. They are becoming increasingly popular and are very cost-effective.

If you buy lots of 'gossip'-type magazines, then consider getting out of this habit to save money – instead, you will find all the same gossip on the internet for free – or get your fix when getting your hair cut, or having a coffee in a café with in-house magazines lying around.

Buying a daily newspaper is a ritual for lots of people, often accompanied with buying a take-away coffee or some pastries. Some people even like carrying it around with them. I don't think I have ever met anyone who read an entire newspaper – some people read only the sports section, others read only the business section – so a lot of people read 10% to 20% maximum of the paper and pay 100% of the price.

Consider getting your sports news or business news online for free, or for a cheap subscription – so you only pay for what you read.

If you go somewhere for a coffee at the weekend or during the week (unless you have taken my advice to make your own coffee and avoid take-aways), very often the good places have daily newspapers available – so why not read them for free while you drink your coffee.

You also will be helping the environment by getting into these habits.

Feed the Birds

Thinking about all your bills can bring up some surprising savings. I was talking recently to a friend of mine, who had started monitoring her bills to look for savings. She realised she had been spending €300 a year on bird food for the birds in her back garden. She had no idea it was costing this much until she tracked the spending.

She stopped buying bird food, but continues to feed the birds with some suitable left-overs from her own meals, stale bread, etc. So the birds continue to be fed, and she will have saved almost €1,000 over the next three years by changing this simple habit.

9: Transport

My Annual Savings: €300

Cars

Buying a Car

The first question when it comes to buying a car is whether to buy new or second-hand. Buying new is always more expensive as up to 50% of the value of a new car is lost in the first three years. However, if no-one bought new cars, then this would lead to serious supply problems, and there will always be customers who buy new and feel it is worth the money.

Buying second-hand involves several options, the main two options being to buy from a garage or to buy privately. If you have a car you need to trade in, then going to a garage is the easiest option. Alternatively, you could sell your car privately, and then either buy from a garage with a discount for no trade-in, or buy privately.

In general, the cheapest option is to buy privately, as when dealing directly with the owner of the car, it is easier to negotiate and there are no middlemen or expensive showrooms to pay for. Buying from a dealer without a trade-in also can yield some good discounts.

Tips for buying new are:

- Watch the option list – they will add little to the second-hand value of the car, maybe 10% of the original options price at most.
- Ensure you are not getting the previous season's model, at the current season's price.
- Consider buying at the end of a month, or quarter, when the salesmen will be anxious to add a final sale to their sales figures.
- Shop around for the best deal.
- Though not new – consider buying a demo model a few months old for a good discount.

Tips for buying privately include:

- Insist on meeting at the owner's house. You can tell a lot about the car from the owner, and the owner's house, as to whether they looked after the car or not.
- Try to turn up a little earlier than announced, so that you get a chance to start the car from cold.
- Bring a friend when going for a test drive with a stranger.
- Get a finance check done on the car and consider a mechanic's inspection unless you are very knowledgeable about cars.

- Research the price of the car you are buying online, to make sure you are not paying too much for it – most people selling a car privately think it is worth more than it actually is.

In general, buying privately is a good option provided you have a reasonable knowledge of cars.

Fuel Type

Currently there are several ways to power a car:

- Petrol: this is the most expensive fuel usually, and not very efficient. Petrol cars are usually the cheapest. If your mileage is low, then a small petrol engine car is a good choice.
- Diesel: this is less expensive than petrol generally, and a lot more efficient. Diesel cars are more expensive than petrol cars, also they are a little noisier but not a lot. They are particularly good on long journeys as opposed to urban use. If your mileage is higher than average, then diesel is a good choice.
- Hybrid: this is a combination of petrol / electric or diesel / electric and is very efficient. Hybrid cars are a little more expensive than the petrol or diesel equivalent but are completely silent when running only on the electric motor. Hybrid engines are run on electric-only in urban driving conditions with lots of stop / start and low speeds. However, on longer journeys outside cities and towns, it is mainly the petrol / diesel engine that is used, so if your driving is

primarily urban or even 50 / 50 urban / extra-urban, then hybrid is the best option.

- Electric: electric-only vehicles are becoming more common. This is the cheapest way to power a car; however, currently there are only a few models available, which are expensive and limited in their range. Again, they are more suited to urban conditions than long journeys on the open road. Charging points are not very common but this is improving. However, in the future, there will be more of a shift towards electric vehicles. There also can be tax incentives for buying an electric car but watch out for hidden costs – for example, some makes of electric cars require the battery to be 'rented' for an annual fee so check out the fine print, as usual.

If you are thinking of trading up your current inefficient car to a more efficient diesel or hybrid, then don't forget the term 'false economy'. This is where you spend a lot of money to buy a newer, more efficient car that is cheaper to run, yet it could take 10 years to save as much as it cost you to change cars – by which time your 'new' car is worth very little. So, if your current car is going quite well, then it may actually be cheaper overall to keep it for another few years, and only change it when it gives trouble and justifies changing. Environmentally speaking, holding on to your current car may be better also given how much energy is used to produce your new 'green' car, and how much energy is used in the disposal of your old car.

Servicing

Servicing is a necessary part of car ownership and, very often, it can be an expensive part that car salesmen never tell you about.

All new cars come with a manufacturer's warranty ranging from three to seven years, depending on the make of car. In general, your warranty is not valid unless you get the car serviced at the main dealer. An increasing number of cars now come with a three-year or five-year 'service inclusive' option, which is well worth getting. So, with new cars there is little you can do to save on servicing apart from buying a service inclusive option.

In the case of older cars where the warranty has expired, it is worth learning some car maintenance skills. The basics like changing wiper blades, light bulbs and air filter are very easy to do. Moving onto the next level – changing the oil and filter, spark plugs, etc. – is quite easy once you've done it once or twice. There are lots of helpful short video demonstrations online for doing these basic service jobs.

You will make significant savings by doing the basic servicing yourself, and your national car test or MOT will do a more thorough check on your car. Most countries have a yearly or two-yearly test, which is done on older cars, to check the road-worthiness and safety features of your car – so it is a useful way to get your car checked. You don't really need to get a garage to check it out prior to the test – if you fail the test, the fee for the re-test is a lot less than getting your car checked in a garage.

What I Did

We have two cars, both outside the manufacturer's warranty, so I carry out the basic servicing on these cars.

The tasks I carry out include changing wiper blades, light bulbs, air filter, oil change, oil filter, spark plugs and topping up all fluids. I buy parts from the main dealers (though I could get spurious parts cheaper from a local motor factors shop but I prefer to use the original parts).

The saving I make is on the labour costs. I generally carry out a service on both cars once a year, which would cost approximately €150 per car on labour – this saves us €300 per year.

Annual Savings: €300

Tyres / Parts

Tyres are also a necessary part of car ownership but there are some ways to reduce this expense:

- Check your tyre pressures every two weeks. If they are too high, the tyres will wear in the middle; if too low, the tyres will wear on the outsides. Having the incorrect pressure in your tyres causes a significant safety hazard also as you have less rubber on the road, hence less grip. Tyre pressure should be checked when the tyres are cold – first thing in the morning or when the car has not been driven in a few hours. The recommended pressures are in the owner manual, and sometimes displayed on the car where the door opens. I bought a good quality tyre pump that plugs into the cigarette lighter, with a digital meter for accurate pressure readings.

- Rotate your tyres every six months. This will result in all four tyres wearing evenly and, when the time comes to change, you may get a better deal by buying four tyres instead of two.

- Driving style significantly affects tyre wear; hard braking, hard acceleration and cornering all result in rapid tyre wear.

- If any of your tyres are wearing on the inside only, or outside only, then the tracking needs to be adjusted in a garage. You can check this on a straight road to see whether the car is dragging to the right or left – this indicates the tracking needs to be looked at.

There are lots of different tyre brands to choose from. Prices vary from very cheap to top of the range and expensive. Very cheap tyres are often bad quality and, as a result, will wear quickly and require much longer distances to stop when braking in an emergency or in the wet. Top of the range, expensive tyres may be designed for performance driving, high speed cornering, etc. For most people, a happy medium is both safe and cost-effective.

Driving Style

Your driving style greatly impacts the fuel consumption of your car:

- Put simply, acceleration uses fuel. Most cars use no fuel when coasting – slowing down with your foot completely off the accelerator.

- If you see a delay, or red lights, ahead then slow down gradually. Maybe you do not need to actually stop and instead can keep the momentum of the car going.

- Try to maintain a constant speed; if you have cruise control on a long journey, this is very fuel-efficient.

- Carrying excess weight in the boot increases fuel consumption also; if there is anything in the boot you do not need, then remove it.

- Driving with a roof-rack also increases fuel consumption; if you are not using it, then remove it from the car.

- Filling your fuel tank when refuelling means you do not have to go to the garage as often – however, unless you do a lot of driving, it will be cheaper to half fill your tank all the time as, on average, this will mean you are driving 50% of the time with approximately 30kg less weight in the car.

- Driving at higher speeds uses more fuel, so refrain from excessive speeds to get better economy.

Other simple driving styles tips include closing all windows, and only using climate control and other ancillaries like the rear window heater when really necessary.

Read through the owner's manual for your car as this will outline the best driving style for your car. Find out from the manual the rpm range where most torque is available and then drive within that range – this means you are making most use of the engine's power.

Driving less is the best way to save fuel, so try to avoid unnecessary journeys or try to get several things done in the same journey.

Flights

Everyone now knows that they should check out fares from low-cost airlines when booking flights.

Use one of the flight comparison websites to find the cheapest flights available to your destination – you may be amazed at the range of options available, including some routes / airlines you may never have considered.

Also clear the cache on your browser (check online help if you do not know how to do this) to clear cookies after each visit to an airline website. Otherwise, the site may take your return visits as an indication of greater interest and bump up prices!

Public Transport

The best way to make savings in public transport is buy monthly or annual tickets, if you use it regularly. This will work out cheaper than paying as you go – and save you the nuisance of having the exact change for fares each time.

10: Entertainment

My Annual Savings: €600

Vacations

Package holidays often can be more expensive than organising the holiday yourself. Investigate the cost of booking flights and accommodation separately – it may save you money. There are several websites where you can deal directly with apartment owners. It is possible to negotiate a better price when dealing with the owners.

If you do decide to go for a package holiday, then look out for half-board or full-board options. These will save you a lot compared to going to restaurants.

Keep an eye out for air fare sales. Also fares are generally cheaper the earlier in advance you book your flights.

House swaps can be a great source of saving on accommodation costs on holidays – with the added advantage of having the full range of household facilities available to you and your family. On a wet day, the extra space of a house over a mobile home or tent really is noticeable! You need to sign up with a house swap /

exchange site and pay their fee to access the database of other people who want to swap. There's lots of advice online.

What I Did

We had just returned from a one-week apartment holiday in Portugal, booked through a travel agent, at a cost for flights and accommodation of €1,900.

We liked it so much that we decided to go again the following year. So, within days of returning, I booked flights almost a year ahead and got a great price for the advance booking. I also did some research online and found an identical apartment, in the same complex, for rent. The total cost was €1,300 – saving us €600 for the same holiday!

Note: The travel agent did provide transport to/from the airport but we had to rent a car anyhow.

Total Annual Savings: €600

Restaurants

Here are some simple ways to make savings on restaurant prices:

- Check whether the restaurant has an early bird menu – if you arrive towards the end of this time, you can still get the cheaper menu yet end up going out for a meal at almost the same time as usual.
- Some restaurants allow you to bring your own wine.
- In the interests of your diet, and to save money, consider sharing the dessert with your partner.

- Check some of the online voucher websites as there are often special offers for restaurants in your area.
- If you are tempted by some of the specials that the waiter mentions to you, but are not on the menu – then don't be afraid to ask how much they are – some restaurants do not mention the price and often the specials not on the menu can be more expensive.
- Shop around for good value restaurants.

11: Principles & Practice

As you read through this book, you may have noted some 'principles' that reoccur again and again. They are basic truths of sensible spending (often no more than commonsense) that apply all the time, every time in every situation.

These principles are:

- Shop around / do price comparisons.
- Think long-term / total cost of use / ownership.
- Think of cumulative, not once-off, savings.
- Pay only for what you need – do a needs analysis.
- Buy in bulk.
- Avoid brands.
- Time your purchases for special / seasonal offers.
- Plan your shopping / avoid impulse buying.
- Learn to DIY – food / cooking, gardening, housekeeping, building repairs, etc.

- Use vouchers / coupons / reward points, etc.
- Track your spending / monitor trends and changes.

If you follow these principles, you will find new ways to apply them to reduce your cost of living without reducing your standard of living – to cut your spending, not your lifestyle – the aim of this book. Depending on your income levels, you should be able to save €5,000 (or pounds or dollars or whatever currency you use wherever you live) each year. And these savings will add up over time to give a cumulative effect. The key is to track your spending and watch your savings build up.

What I Did

In each chapter of this book, I have shown how I saved money in a variety of different ways. I have told you exactly how much I saved. I have been doing this for the past three years and I'm now on year four of savings!

In summary, my savings in a typical year are shown in the table on the next page.

So now it's over to you. Best of luck!

		€
Housing	Mortgage	1,000
Utilities	Electricity	300
	Gas	400
	Phone	300
	Cable TV	60
	Refuse collection	84
Food	Groceries	1,250
	At work / Snacks	1,081
Children	Rechargeable Batteries	150
Banking & Personal Finance	Fees	240
	Credit card	30
Insurance	Car	100
	House	103
	Mortgage protection	408
	Travel	75
Personal & Household	Barber / hairdresser	260
Transport	Car servicing	300
Entertainment	Holidays	600
TOTAL ANNUAL SAVINGS		**6,741**

About the Author

James O'Donovan has a B.Sc. in Computer Science and a Post Graduate Diploma in Computer Engineering.

He spent the first eight years of his career working in software development for several Irish and international software companies and the past 11 years working in the area of Information System Compliance and Validation of Computerised Systems for many of the multinational pharmaceutical companies in Ireland.

He has always had a keen interest in getting value for money and sourcing good deals for anything he purchases. He is particularly interested in helping people to spend their money smarter in the current recessionary climate.

In his spare time, he enjoys running, cooking, keeping up-to-date with the latest advances in the world of motoring and reading anything in the area of entrepreneurship and innovation.

He is married to Rosaleen and has one son, Daniel.

Visit James's website at **www.HowToSave5000.com**.

HowToSave5000.com

Visit the website to register for more information to help you to manage your savings on an ongoing basis, as easily as possible.

You can save money straightaway by signing up for my online **HowToSave5000** course – just quote the code **HTS5000** to get a discount!

Follow me on twitter **@HowToSave5000** and read my blog on the website.

Feel free to contact me – details are available on the Contact page of the website.

Save 40% on the HowToSave5000 online course

Sign up for my online **HowToSave5000** course and save €20 – more than double the cost of this book – immediately. Just quote the code **HTS5000** to get your discount!

The course covers the nine spending areas in this book – in more detail, with specific recommendations and constantly-updated tips and techniques. And you can track your savings online as you make them, building up to your target of €5,000.

Signing up for the course saves you double the cost of this book – and will help you to save hundreds of times more. Don't delay! Sign up at **www.HowToSave5000.com** and start saving now!

OAK TREE PRESS

Oak Tree Press develops and delivers information, advice and resources for entrepreneurs and managers. It is Ireland's leading business book publisher, with an unrivalled reputation for quality titles across business, management, HR, law, marketing and enterprise topics. NuBooks is its recently-launched imprint, publishing short, focused ebooks for busy entrepreneurs and managers.

In addition, through its founder and managing director, Brian O'Kane, Oak Tree Press occupies a unique position in start-up and small business support in Ireland through its standard-setting titles, as well as training courses, mentoring and advisory services.

Oak Tree Press is comfortable across a range of communication media – print, web and training, focusing always on the effective communication of business information.

Oak Tree Press, 19 Rutland Street, Cork, Ireland.
T: + 353 21 4313855 F: + 353 21 4313496.
E: info@oaktreepress.com W: www.oaktreepress.com.